IT'S A POET'S TREE

IT'S A POET'S TREE

consonant

copyright page

This book is entirely a work of fiction. The names, characters and incidents portrayed in it are the product of the author's imagination. Any resemblance to actual persons, living or dead, or events or localities is entirely coincidental.

Paperback Edition May 21, 2025
ISBN 979-8899611118-6

"It's a poet's Tree. It is a Poetry."

"*Power comes to them, who aim the best.*"

PREFACE

"it's a poet's tree" is not just a play on words—it is a space I return to, where thoughts branch out into verse, and emotions take root in metaphor. This tree has grown quietly within me, fed by moments of silence, wonder, and reflection.

Many of these poems were written in the blurred margins of day and night—often typed on a phone, often in a rush to catch a fleeting feeling. But they carry within them more than just emotion. My background in physics and mathematics naturally seeped into the lines—sometimes as metaphors, sometimes as structure, and sometimes as the very rhythm of thought. After all, the universe speaks in equations, but it aches in poetry.

These poems are not answers, but questions left open about love, time, longing, light, and distance. About why a falling apple matters, and why it still hurts. About gravity, not just of planets, but of the heart.

If this collection offers you a place to pause, to feel, or to think a little deeper about the invisible forces that move us—then the tree has done its work.

These poems are leaves of my inner tree—each one shaped by love, silence, longing, and the ever-changing seasons of life. Some carry the fragrance of childhood, others the ache of parting. Many were written in the quiet corners of the day, when the heart spoke in whispers and the world didn't interrupt.

To me, poetry is both sanctuary and surrender. In these lines, I have tried to hold on to what slips away—faces, feelings, fragments of dreams. There's nothing grand here, only honesty. No proclamations, only presence.

I would like to thank Parijat Goswami and Swarup Lal Saha for their valuable insights.

If even one poem in this tree offers you shade, fruit, or a breeze of recognition, then this little forest of words has found its purpose.

With gratitude and a quiet heart,
Sabyasachi Ray
Cooch Behar

Contents

01. Quantum Grief — 1

02. Stars & Us — 2

03. A Quiet Release — 3

04. My Religion — 4

05. Which Path To Choose — 5

06. Love Bleeds — 6

07. Force of Attraction — 7

08. The Spring of My Heart — 8

09. Love in a Multiverse — 9

10. Not to Be in Love — 10

11. Illusion of Love — 11

12. Accidental Poet — 12

13. Consonant — 13

14. Scientific Relation   14

15. Heart of Stone   15

16. Toxic Man   16

17. Weed   17

18. The Sin of Loving You   18

19. An Ant on A Leaf   19

20. Or you can   20

21. Loved & Dead   22

22. Withdrawal Symptoms   23

23. Take It Easy   24

24. The Vanishing Path   25

25. I Let You Free   26

26. The Casanova   28

27. The Ghost   29

28. Soul Touch   30

29. Cherished Hope   31

30. Heart Got Hurt   32

31. Intentions for A Sidewalk   33

32. What's Alive Within 34

33. A Dream in Slow Mo 35

34. My Favourite Pen 36

35. Sole Sufferer 37

36. Universe & Me 38

37. Whisper 39

38. Never Stop Trying 40

39. The Scars 41

40. Purpose of Life 43

41. Maverick 44

42. The Timing Was Wrong 46

43. Life's Integral Calculus 47

44. A Spring Night 48

45. Love Break, I Break Love 49

46. In Every Breath 50

47. Sudden Awake 51

48. What Loving Is 52

49. The Park 53

50. Justice and Warrant   54

51. The Poet's Tree   56

52. I Am Not A Poet   57

53. Deep Sink in Your Heart   58

54. You Won't Find Me   59

55. Eternal One   60

56. Time to Unlove   61

57. All Goodbyes Are Not from The Heart   62

58. Why The Fire Broke in The Wood?   64

59. Miss You   65

60. Damaged Phone   66

61. Green Flags, Red Rinses   67

62. Mother Earth   68

63. Once I Was Lost in Babylon   69

64. I Am Lucifer   71

65. No Reason for Love   72

66. Jean Tatlock   73

67. Mark Antony & Cleopatra   74

68. The Solitude of Sorrow 76

69. A Mid-Summer Day Dream 77

70. Pain 78

71. Nothing, Only Pain 80

72. Stardust Pilgrim 81

73. Alien Expression 83

74. A Beautiful Moment 84

75. Cigarette 85

76. Nature as The Messenger 86

77. Your Happiness is Mine 87

78. The Dilemma of Dual Love 88

79. None Left Without Hope 89

80. You Vanquished Everything of Me 91

81. Separation and Separation 93

82. The Lost Snow White 94

83. Universe 96

84. Every Show Must Go On 97

85. Love is The Only Reason to Grow 98

86. Love With a Fall   99

"Why do we die? To make life precious…"-somewhere
    in the vacuum   100

QUANTUM GRIEF

The pain inside me
may be measured in quanta,
but it lies in a continuum—
so intense, so grief-stricken,
yet so asymptotic.

I cannot hold it right,
unable to overcome.
The uncertainty of measuring
position and momentum
was never precise.

So it is, and so it will remain
throughout my manifest.
Someday, I must be extinct,
and find myself recovered—complete—
in a state of quantum superposition,
wrapping up every possible duality.

Stars & Us

Under the stars,
you and I
start growing together.
we
are getting older
as the stars glow brighter.

A Quiet Release

Everything fell apart,
like a storm tearing through the forest,
dreams shattered in the darkness,
hopes lost in a silent street.

But from the ruins,
a calmness grew —
a quiet release,
now the chaos is gone,
and there is peace.

My Religion

I am Hindu, so is Asifa.
Asifa is Muslim, I am too.
Coz we both belongs to mankind,
we are Christian too.

WHICH PATH TO CHOOSE

Between street and avenue,
I have to choose the street.
Though, I loved the avenue one.

Between love and let you go,
I have to choose both.
Because, I can't choose either.
Alvida

Love Bleeds

Stars that glitter much die sooner.
Your love was the brightest star
in the Eden of my heart.
So, I can't hold you long.
You have
taken away every single beat.
Thus, heart stopped being normal.

Outburst is the fate of a dying star.
But it doesn't fade away alone,
it suffers a lot of steps and pains
to destroy itself and co-existence.

It wasn't a normal one.
The Devine love bleeds greater.
So much pain and emptiness,
allows us to evaporate in a void forever.

FORCE OF ATTRACTION

With a delicate heart,
I am standing in front of the event horizon.
Lights bent thus,
I can see my past and future.
All senses are eager
to take me to the singularity.
Where time may pause forever,
or I can lose you eternal.
The pull of gravitation is extreme here,
still not enough to fight with the one,
that pulled me towards her.

All my memories accreted
around the sphere of compactness.
Erasing all slowly with the emission of bright photons,
that might reach you one day.
And you will be light-kissed
with memories of my evaporation.

The Spring of My Heart

Beautiful ixora flower in full bloom,
breezes touch them to get inhaled.
The shower of flame of the forest,
has softened my avenue with red velvet.
Royal poincianas standing still on both sides,
radiating beauty all around.
The fragrance of crape Jasmine,
felt like heaven within.
The Spring of my heart,
always filled with the most beautiful flowers.
Spring is the season of life forever.

LOVE IN A MULTIVERSE

In a thousand lifetimes,
in various multiverse,
I have found you.
Every time we passed by,
cosmic waves rippled the fabric of the space-time.
I remember in some places you killed me.
We were unhappy together in some universe.
Even in some universes, we were just friends of friends.
In a few we were rivals.
Never been so happy.
Never been so close.
But there is a universe across millions of worm holes apart,
where you and I are remembered forever.
For the sacrifices, for the pains of love
we suffered.
That consciousness of love is spread over
all the parallel universes.
To compensate for that love,
I killed you somewhere,
you killed me elsewhere.
But we both felt deep regret killing us both.
And that process of love
will keep happening for millions of times,
in millions of multiverses.

Not to Be in Love

Thank you for loving me.
Your love has conspired to meet my inner me.
I can see how much common I am to the others?
How much selfish and self-centred!
My every act of love has hurt you so much,
that pain is unbearable to my shattered heart of glass.
It was me who tried to cage your love with emotions.
But forgot there is no place of a cage in love.
Now I see myself in a cage,
sitting lonely beside a river,
that sings the saddest melancholy written ever.
To free myself,
I have to make you free.
I have to give your heart wings to fly.
Thus, only I will survive
and perhaps happy to see you happy again.

ILLUSION OF LOVE

No trace of water droplets that fall in a desert from the
heaven remains long.
So is the pain.
It is never ending.
Still, no one will ever essence it other than self.

No darkness can ever block the path of light.
So is the heart.
It will never forget to beat until the end.

No moon ever can meet its sun,
unless it's eclipse.
In eclipse at least it feels like they are together,
although it's just an illusion.

So is the illusion of love.
Everyone just felt,
none experienced.
Told by many
tried by few,
with a fate of failure and misery.

Accidental Poet

I have nothing to do.
This nothingness compels me to write.
I write nothing but abstract and absurd.
Still, those black lines on white pages,
becomes my sign of presence.

Some time it becomes the monument of love,
Sometimes just a grave yard for broken heart.
It changes its shape, meanings, emotions
over the passage of time.
The only thing that I have to offer
to the world is-
"A Few words".

CONSONANT

Consonant is no one.
Does nothing.
Creates abstract and absurd.
Amongst the alphabet consonants are the majority.
So is the case for the author,
he is a very common person.
Close to your heart.
You can read him
and feel as if it is your own writing.
The name itself signifies
that very commonness.

SCIENTIFIC RELATION

We are in a relation,
No mathematical equation can express.
No theorem is solid enough to
explain the feeling we both share.
No experiment can be done
to verify the closeness or separation we keep.
Our internal longing is not governed by any rule.
Our whispered desires defy all the laws of nature.
Heartfelt yearning cannot be measured in units.
Unspoken admiration cannot be experienced,
by any instruments.
Only the romantic murmur creates reverberation,
in the fabric of the cosmos in different dimensions
and fluttering tales of our desire propagate
among the cosmic dwellers.

HEART OF STONE

No one needs love nowadays
It's ancient
It's pure
Nowadays times are more valuable than care
Money is more valuable than empathy
Physic is more valuable than the soul

Sometimes unearthed one comes
To stay with us
To get loved
But returns to void
With heavy hearts.
Thus, a stone heart is born

Toxic Man

Every time you come to me,
my heart melts.
I am a toxic man.
As I melt,
become more poisonous.
That pours into your veins,
and absorbed in your blood.
If you consume me,
perhaps therapy will be a remedy,
to turn you back to life.
If you inhale me,
you will lose your consciousness
and thrive to survive.
The only way, I know is –
to make you happy forever,
make you stay away from me.
it's heartbreaking,
but still, I can, For you, my love.
It's better to lose you happy
than keeping close to me,
with toxic rewards.
It's so painful, my love
I must not hold you long,
because I am a toxic man,
whose love can give you
only scars and broken hearts.

WEED

In a field wrapped in bamboo leaves,
from the dusky heart
within the pure white body of the crape jasmine,
A message of smoke
etched itself into my mind.

It still lingers.
Moment after moment,
the celestial bliss of slumber and wakefulness
has kept me
enchanted to this day.

The Sin of Loving You

I know that everything was, is, and will remain
meaningless to you.
Yet I alone know how real it was.
Yes, the magnetic field of your eyes
has cast a Zeeman effect upon my heart.
Because of you,
I have wandered through illusions—
Beautiful mirages that became a part of me,
lingering in the silent corridors of time.

It was you who led me to touch
the flowers of grass,
to pluck false strawberries
from their delicate stems.

The sin I committed was loving you—
and now, I must pay the price.

Now, legitimately,
it's time to pay back for my sins.
You are the reason I once danced with joy,
beneath the layered embrace of sky, birds, and trees.
Yet now, I see—
There is a kenón at the heart of creation.
I deserve misery, pain, sorrow, and suffering.

I deserve a great fall—
and for each fall,
I cannot make gravity alone responsible.

An Ant on A Leaf

A leaf old and yellow,
fell off the branches on a stream of flow.

Ripples of water carried it to the river,
an ant was perhaps trying to cipher.

On the way through the Forrest and valley,
the ant got some time to rest on its belly.

Auto phobia strikes the head of the ant in melancholy,
it tried to use the breeze to divert the leaf to some meadowly.

At the very end of the tour leaf strikes a green field,
the ant thanked the pale leaf
for letting him take refuge and journey to another land
where food and shelter lay unveiled.

OR YOU CAN

Don't forget me
(Or you can!)
I have to go with the wind
But never think I am gone.

Don't forgive me
(Or you can!)
I had to stay calm and listen a lot
But never think I agreed at all

Baby! Don't punish me
(Or you can!)
I might play not like a pro
But never think I am a naive

Don't ever blame me
(Or you can!)
I had thousand reasons to state
But never think I am going to explain.

Mi Amor!
I can see, but I won't watch
I can speak, but I won't talk
I can feel, but I won't touch
I can have affection, but I won't love

Don't dislike me
(Or you can!)
I might not that good

Never think me good.

21

Never think me good.

Loved & Dead

I am afraid
Storms in my head
No bills to be paid
I am dismayed
Never loved
And never hated
Sometime I played
Every time failed
Finally laid
Because I am dead
And no one cried

WITHDRAWAL SYMPTOMS

congratulations
You have overcame me.
Perhaps I was the drug supplier
and now you have stopped taking those pills.
It's fine,
it will keep your heart and soul
fit and fine.

I'm happy for you,
besides sad for me.
It took a lot,
it was too expensive,
harvesting drug for you.

Your healing pills,
needed my blood to spill
and veins to stretch,
continuous injections to my heart's abode.

Now,
I must take a long vacation,
but heart will Keep processing drugs.
As no one left to receive,
self-consumption
might just make it stop.

That's right.

TAKE IT EASY

It is not as complex as quantum physics,
rather it is simple as photons.
It is not as vast as Atlantic,
rather calm and tiny as kapotakkhi.
It is not as scorching as summer noon,
rather comfortable as tranquil evening.
It is not as tremendous as storm,
rather soothing like breeze.
It is not as sinister as grin,
rather radiant like smile.
It is not as tedious as writing a poem,
rather it is captivating like dance.
It is not as cruel as death,
rather soft as heartbreak!
It is not as hard as incomplete,
as easy as happy endings.

THE VANISHING PATH

Hailstorm rages, the frozen breeze bites,
the sea roars wild in the heart of the night.
Waves rise high, erasing my trail, only random stones,
while whispers in woods looming terror into the bones.

Steps sink deep in the grasp of the sand,
lightning strikes where birches stand.
Fallen trees, fire's cruel embrace,
seal my path in a burning maze.

A sentinel mountain, a demon in black,
watches my journey, forcing me back.
Flowers now thorns, sharp and unkind,
piercing the road I'm destined to find.

Even time has ceased to flow,
the Creator conspires, whispering "No."
All roads to you—lost in the air,
vanished, hidden—despair."

I Let You Free

Wish
I had never met you
Wish
I had never felt you
Wish
I never loved you

Reason is not
That I have no feelings left
Reason is not
That I am angry over you
Reason is not
That I no more love you

Rather
I am in a paradox
Rather
I am sad over losing you
Rather
I want you forever

Still
I can not give you your pride
Still
I can not stay with you forever
Still
I have to lose someday

That is why

I prefer let you free.

The Casanova

In a casa blanca,
once reside a Casanova.
Who wove tales in whispers,
by moonlight and aroma.

With roses in hand and a spellbinding smile,
he footed through hearts, to win by mile.

Silken words like a poet's tale,
left lovers lost where silence fell.

Yet in his eyes,
a longing persists all above,
for the bella he loved,
with love, which was stronger than love.

THE GHOST

With the mist and the moist
I wrote a story.
At the dawn it became a ghost
and it was in hurry.

Will-o-the-wisp
travelling all over and cry.
Ghost rush and whisper in crisp
I just on your back, the firefly.

You turn around your face
and find yourself in complete grace.
you see me, dash
but in a while, I turned in to ash.

Ash was blown away by the sudden flood of dark water.
Everything was clear and bare bright, thereafter.

Soul Touch

I can touch your lips
even after the separation you choose
Because, I never touched
Your beautiful lips
With my fingers or lips.
I touched them with my heart and soul
So, I can touch thee afar and forever.
I wish I could hold you long
But it's love
So, I accept what you want.

You may call incomplete,
But I possess you
Fully inside me.
I can hug myself now,
No one to judge thou.

CHERISHED HOPE

Cloud showers over me
Every night.
Kiss of the moon
fades in flight.

I know you try
to hold me tight.
But I have to suffer
the toughest battle I fight.

Sometimes words
don't come out right.
Even nature
compels us to fright.

Still, I cherish
your gentle sight.
Hoping one day
our sky will shine bright.

Dreaming about those days and nights
I find my heart in complete delight.

Heart Got Hurt

Believe or leave me.
I might not fight or fright.
That doesn't mean,
I don't have a heart
or
I don't get hurt.

I am not a knight
Even not in the night
That doesn't mean,
I must cry
or
I ll give you my heart's fry

It's true that I can't forget
Also, I can't let you recollect
That doesn't mean,
I ll follow your way
or
Beg you to stay

INTENTIONS FOR A SIDEWALK

Why are you going back?
Why I am trying to not stop you?
You know it won't give you right track
I know I won't be happy without you.

Still, I have reasons to stop myself,
but, you!
You have the opportunity to make a new world
maybe not with me.
But here in this beautiful pasture land
of love and moisture.
You could have a happier life.
Where I might not be a part,
still may found you always
through breeze, through the highway.
Through the grasses, through the fallen leaves,
under the tree behind your home, or
on a sidewalk of your town.

I am sure I will be able to feel you
closely even if you are far.
Still, I long for your presence
In my small corazón.
Hoping to see you by accidents
that will happen very often.
I don't fear over loosing you,
I fear one day I will loose my adobe in your heart.

What's Alive Within

Reviewing my inner self,
I found something beyond time.
Truth and daring,
Unbound love for you.
Perhaps, the infinity created
And nurtured by light and dust.
Rejuvenating attraction and desire,
Never ending love and longing,
Always alive within.

A Dream in Slow Mo

I see you walking,
walking toward me—
Forever,
In a never-ending loop.

This infinite approach—
It was beautiful,
it was hope.
But as time rushes like a stream,
it has begun to haunt me.

It was never an eternal distance,
yet time, perhaps, has folded in—
Or is it just a trick
of illusions within me?
Did you never start?
Or have you already arrived?

Whatever the truth may be,
the melancholies in me
will linger forever.
Someone must bury them
in the graveyard with mine.

My Favourite Pen

My favourite pen.
Always kept in my book pocket.
As it stays close to my heart,
it has its heartbeat now.

Though it is induced one.
Still, the words came out of it,
is quite a great replicate of my thoughts.
Smooth and gentle black strikes on white paper
engraves me for retrospect in future.

SOLE SUFFERER

The water
and the rusted nail.
The Storm
and the uprooted woodland giant.
The drought
and the abyssal wound of the earth.
The fire in the wood
And the burnt deer.
The spring
And the fallen leaf.
The broken egg
And the lost life.

No one cares.
Nothing changes.
Only the two,
one who loose
and the lost
sole sufferers
of the wounds.

Universe & Me

Somewhere between heaven and hell,
Always I tried to climb and fail.
Besides star dusts and galaxies,
Yearning for the truth of universe and me.

Absolutely nothing is filled everywhere,
Sharing melancholic waves of an unknown realm;
Astonishingly calm despite rapid expansion,
Creating a harmony between zero and one.

High and intense cosmic flux
Irradiates existence beyond the elysix.

WHISPER

In the darkest hour.
I heard the whisper.
Sigh of the air Just utter
and left me forever.

She was not your ever,
but loved you more than any other.
You can't see heart is bleeding in her.
still smiling like, just she doesn't care.

Your actions made shattered on her own,
just like lead someone on and let them down.
You can make my words note down,
you must pay the price and get drown.

NEVER STOP TRYING

To the world
After a fall
Being hurt too much
Lied never, still
Eternally destructed

Trying to reshape
Ending all misfortune
Never loosing hope
Never stopped trying
In the process
Situation might change

THE SCARS

The sky above sometimes crumbles down,
like drifting snowflakes and encloses me.
As the pain of the heart deepens,
blue fades into black,
and love disappears—like a poem erased.

For ages, for aeons, I have remained awake,
beside the stars in the darkness.
A shooting star falls into the owl's keen eyes,
perching each night on the ashwatha's branch.

Under the weight of fallen sal leaves,
the garden's grass bears its deep wounds.
ants retreat into the unknown,
marching in lost, endless trails.

One day, in the season of rains,
when the leaves decay and drift away,
the green grass starts to flatter—
Do those who drift ever return?

After the rain, light and light—sharp, piercing,
with claws raised, the shadow of tomorrow lurks.
At life's end, every account is settled,
when every poetry-laden page is torn apart.

In moonlight's glow, all emotions burn,
yet some scars never fade away.
Again and again, they return in the biting cold,

in hues of cotton white, at every newborn dawn.

PURPOSE OF LIFE

Summer is yet to arrive,
full of food and flowers.
Makes a breeding boom.
Not only the animals and birds,
all the insects are also busy now.
Building nests and colonies
pollinating flowers, moving towards migration.
Some are shedding fur,
some seeking sheds and water.
Too much fresh vegetation
and active hunting for the young generation.
Moths and fireflies are getting alive at night.
No time for shedding tears
or space for repairing hearts.
These are too trivial
life has a greater purpose.

MAVERICK

I speak with the dewdrops
and sing along with the breeze.
I blaze like the sun,
and soar with the birds.
I flutter like a restless heart,
yet I spin like the earth.
I am infinite like the boundless sky,
yet lifeless like the inert.
I am certain like the truth,
and radiant like a diamond.

I am restless like a doe,
and eternal like farewell.
Like the lingering trace of an ending,
I remain forever.
I stay awake through the night,
and lie still through the day.
At times, I am a storm,
and at times, I am silent.

I am gentle like the morning,
I am the mystic of a cremation ground.
I am Lucifer,
once divine, now merely human.
With my own hands, I have severed my wings.

I am the compass of a lost sailor,
I am Krishna's flute,
Radha's laughter and ecstasy.

Like the rain, I fall in torrents,
yet remain calm like the past.

I am lifeless,
silent.

The Timing Was Wrong

Everything was just right.
The spring breeze carried a sweet fragrance.
Branches were adorned with blossoms.
Birds sang in joyful chorus.
Piles of fallen leaves had gathered.
Orchids embraced the trellis with love.
The sunlight was soft and warm.
There was laughter, music, and dance.
We met.
There were whispers in the ear.
Hearts trembled with emotions.
Everything was in place.
Only the timing was wrong.

LIFE'S INTEGRAL CALCULUS

I have done all the integrations,
over life,
over space,
and over time.

I had to choose a limit of
emotions,
infinite,
and lifetime.

After all the calculations
and derivations,
results appear
to be non-real, absurd.

In life,
in space,
in time,

There is
no life,
no space,
no time.

What left is only
imaginary numbers.

A Spring Night

Look at the half moon
through the green leaves
slept in the dark gray branches
of rain trees in a late spring.

New leaves are making prominent presence.
Still the branches are dominating
with their spider-like waves.
Sponger spreading all over
few but beautiful buds of
Parasitic plants.

At dark how beautiful that might be.
Incomplete moon lights draw a shade
over my presence of oblivion.
All the pain is swallowed by the branches.
Still a cracking heart yet to resilient

Love Break, I Break Love

She was never meant to stay,
yet loved me more than words could say.
I tore her heart apart,
left a scar, then chose to depart.

Her eyes still make me cry,
how could I break a heart so shy?
Destroying everything, I feel the pain,
how much she suffered—I can't explain.

If I could, I'd go to hell,
bring myself back just to tell—
How could you hurt a heart so kind?
Forlorn by you, how you hope to stay refined?

In Every Breath

I can hear you
in a silent breeze.
I can see you
in the darkest nights.
I can smell you
even in kenos.
I can feel you
in my rhythms.
I can hold you
in my dreams.
I can remember you
in my prayers.
I can bargain for you
in exchange of life.
I can forget you.
Never

Sudden Awake

Sinked in the dark of your eyes
the stream of water
touched the tip of my nose,
and in their wandering
awakened a feeling on our lips.

Neither sweet nor salty,
such infinite sorrow,
such bleeding hearts.

In the maze of right and wrong,
in the unfamiliar scent of night jasmine,
perhaps all our hopes
are now lost and gone.
Neither in rhythm
nor in joy,
yet they will linger forever in my bones.

What Loving Is

If loving you is a crime
I will remain a criminal.
If loving you is a certificate to character
Yes, I have the worst one.
If loving you is illegal
I must be imprisoned forever.
If loving is death warrant
I am happy to perish myself.
You're none to stop me now
I'm not the one you love,
I'm the guilty of loving you.

THE PARK

So many new faces,
small yet radiant,
eager to explore the unknown,
illuminating the park.

They outshine
the palm trees,
neatly spaced along
the avenue stretching through.

Look at them—
Their happiness,
their smiles,
ever ready to breathe
fresh air and vibrant blooms
into any mind.
For every weary soul,
their magic lifts despair,
gone like mist in sunlight.
Happiness forever.

Justice and Warrant

You sought justice for rape,
but never received it.
Does it even matter?

You sought justice for bribery,
but never received it.
Yet the world moved on, unbothered.

You sought justice for theft,
but never received it.
Did it change anything for anyone?

I never asked for a trial of love,
never needed to know,
yet I passed the verdict.

A death sentence—
Perhaps they were already dead,
just gasping for one more breath.
I ended it effortlessly.

No one will have a headache over it,
not now, not ever.
Once it was headache simply because they were happy.

What is love?
Being there.
Is being there the same as love?

What is love?
A feeling of joy.
Is joy the same as love?

Whatever it may be,
they were guilty of wrongdoing.
The warrant has been issued.

Now, they are gone.
No more injustice remains.
The world is green, calm, and serene once more.
No unfulfilled longings remain anymore.

The Poet's Tree

Today, I was there,
under that tree, you know.
I was there with reminiscence,
for merely twenty minutes.
it was heavy, so it felt like an infinite moment.

I left, leaving everything behind,
in hope—I will come back to recollect all.
The tree will stand still,
unless I lose it,
somehow, sometime,
as I have already lost you,
just like in a surge.

I wish I could bathe
in a downpour of tears
and leave the tree forever.

I Am Not A Poet

I am not a poet.
Never I was.
But it's words that
just came out of me,
were loved and written
in random manners,
became a poem.

Chaotic words,
broken thoughts,
scribbled over paper,
took a shape—
Like a paint, not so clear,
it turned into a poem.

It was not a good one,
it was not perfect,
but it cleared the mind.
As words were storming inside—
So much pain,
so much anger—
All just became a poem.

Now you want to take back
everything,
every word,
every pain that you gifted.
Better take my world—
Let the poem stay forever.

Deep Sink in Your Heart

You know how much you mean to me.
I am in deep sink in your heart.
Hope you can feel me in your heartbeats.
I know I am in your veins and cells in your brain.
I am confident that
you are surrounded by all the memories created by us.
I am sure you can't arise from our hangover.
I know because
I'm already in a state of void made by us.

YOU WON'T FIND ME

One day will come

You won't find me
in the grass flowers,
or under the rain tree
in springs sweet fall,
or in hottest summer.

You won't find me
in the corridors,
or in the seat besides,
in the car,
or in the path to home.

You will never find me
in the birds song,
or in your dream,
in the rain,
or in the pain.

I wish I could,
then I must would
clean your heart and
erase myself from
where (your heart) I reside.

Eternal One

The grain of sand that fell by the Arabian Sea,
or the stone of Egypt's pyramids,
perhaps in the caves of an ancient mountain,
or in the flesh stuck to a dinosaur's tooth,
sometimes within the waters of the Nile,
or maybe in the body of some distant planet,
or in the flames of a comet's fire.
It could have been on Noah's Ark,
or deep within the Earth's molten core.

Even before the birth of Earth,
the planets, the stars,
and this vast, infinite universe,
the tiny particles that once existed—
They are the ones that formed you and me.
Perhaps they were right beside each other,
So close, fused as one,
Just as far as you and I are now.

TIME TO UNLOVE

I need time to unlove you.
Maybe that of one eternity.
I need distances to travel to unlove you.
May be a distance of a million parsec.
I need to crush myself to unlove you.
Maybe a load of a thousand mountains.
I need to fuse myself to unlove you.
Perhaps a zillion nuclear fusion might do so.
I have to break my heart to unlove you.
But this much breaking would not suffice.
I have to cross the boundaries to unlove you.
But the border of life and death, beyond my wish.

All Goodbyes Are Not from The Heart

How can I not disturb you
How can I not look at you
How can I not talk to you

You are not doing great
being alone.
You are not looking happy
anymore.

I can see
your eyes are always looking for me
I can feel
your heart is beating for me
I can hear
my name in your silent etch

So how can you be so sure
I am not for you anymore
Why are you trying to say goodbye?

Now how can I live without
How can I smile without
How can I feel without

Tell my why and
how should I
forget everything, every wish, every time

in between us.

Why The Fire Broke in The Wood?

Why the fire broke in the wood?
Is it the scorching heat,
or the venomous air,
or the poor woods itself?
No one to judge, none to blame.

Still, the ash and the flame,
the smoke and the tars
remind the sorrows of massacre.

Rains came — tremendous and turbulent —
They swept all the traces,
pains and devastations.

Only thing left: the dark land.
Once, it was evergreen and serene.
Day by day, gentle moisture
will love the air and sun.
Fertile land — even better than ever —
Will cover the void with prosperous green.
No one to remember, none to tell.

MISS YOU

When night ends,
the stars in the sky fade away,
the long, wandering rivers lose their way,
they answer no call,
no voice, no plea,
the wind flows on—
like the stream of destiny.
Someone, it seemed,
had called in the night,
but all remains undone, beyond my sight.
Washed away by rain,
memories adrift—unclear,
as the last light dies,
the soul draws near.
In the address of my heart,
I find only me—
missing you, my dear.

Damaged Phone

Uncountable memories chronicle
all stored in my mobile.
Broken display, no response to touch
those were important, too much.

It was better, if it was dead.
No pain of hope should have stayed.
But it's on all day and night long
unable to scroll reminisces, tried so strong.

Once it swallowed everything of me.
Now, no answer, just reflecting me.
Cracks on top of the wallpaper
just smiles like salt and pepper.

This isn't all the pain I bear:
They stopped making the display—
I can't transfer, can't repair,
nothing works. It stays that way.

GREEN FLAGS, RED RINSES

Everything is perfect,
and everything is great.
Contemplating is full of difficulties,
so, stay as it is — and destroy at ease.

Everywhere, darkness
in the dynasty of the Queen;
Society in sickness,
corruption and unclean.

No one is to stand,
and no one is to rise.
Everyone gives praise,
but the poor pays the price.

Here, Witch is the Queen,
and Chimera is the Prince.
Flag of the state is green,
and red drops drip as they rinse.
No one to say "stop" at all —
But still, they fear.
dynasty must fall;
Queen and Prince know mayhem is near.

Mother Earth

Planet Earth revolves, fit and fine,
no matter what we did or will do in future.
Our million lifetimes are just a blink for Earth,
so whatever harm we might've done —
That's to none but us, the humankind.

Even after the extinction of last tree, the last life,
Earth will recover itself to restart.
It is infinite source and infinite sink,
so fertile we can't imagine.

No worry — we can harm as much we like.

ONCE I WAS LOST IN BABYLON

Once I was lost in Babylon,
found myself atop a pyramid,
beside the mighty Euphrates—
No east, no west, no north, no south.

I plunged into pain, into sorrow,
carried downstream by the flow.
Sand and whispers filled my lungs;
I lost all sense—even in dreams.

It was late evening in Mesopotamia,
I found you sitting by my side,
weaving your fingers through my wet hair—
I saw you once… then lost all sight.

So deep, so dark, so still, so calm—
And yet, eyes so full of care.
Your radiant face, your hair in the breeze…
I remember nothing
but eyes that hypnotized.

Floating with time and wind,
I know I'll find you again—
I see your eyes in every dream,
carrying a thousand years of blue.

I swim in fire and drink the air

to see your eyes once more in the imminent—
The deep of your eyes suffocated me.
Is that pain of your heart, or care for me?

I dive deep and swim through your pain,
searching for you across the ages.
In pursuit of losing you—
Again, And again, Forever.

I Am Lucifer

I fell—but not for lust or hate,
nor for a crown, nor twist of fate.
I questioned law, I dared to speak—
And found the heavens cold and bleak.

They called me dark, yet I was flame,
the echo of a sacred name.
A star cast down, yet still I burn—
With truths the silent stars must learn.

I turn the white to ash-stained dark,
I shield mankind from heaven's bark.
Tell them—let fire strip my wings,
still, I will shatter all their kings.

I am Lucifer—angels' love,
who spit on their gifts and thrones above.
I steal their pride, and wear it free;
I dwell where I was meant to be.

Don't ask me how or why I fell—
You heard it once, you know it well:
Better to reign in fire and flame,
than live in heaven without a name.

No Reason for Love

Thousand reasons to leave,
but no reason for love.
If you ask why I love, and how,
you will only find silence— for now.

Perhaps I can explain for separation,
the reason and pain.
It was for the society, the humankind,
for a brighter future you might someday find.

But I can utter almost nothing
while you ask why I have started loving.
If I could — perhaps I should —
But for a reason, love never would.

JEAN TATLOCK

Love is love.
But on earth,
consequences are always bitter.
Loving someone of utmost importance was never better.
Relation, separation—everything like deadlock,
the fate of gorgeous, passionate Jean Tatlock.
Longings—more than longing, for infinite quantum times!
Just a meeting with the desired man, once in a lifetime.
Turmoil, the power, curiosity grows inside spy hearts—
the ending of a beautiful life, accelerated as in a cyclotron.
Whom to hold responsible?
Whom to blame?
Was she dead already by the agony of solitary,
or was she killed by the ignorance of her love?

MARK ANTONY & CLEOPATRA

Beach of Tarsus, sun down orange,
so is the sea, reflecting beauty — pretty one.
Mesmerizing breeze striking the luxurious barge,
much more candid, like goddess Aphrodite on golden
mirage.

It hypnotizes him — tension, fear, war on a sudden,
turned into peace, calm, admiration.
No negotiations — Cleopatra's aura was so charming,
Mark Antony could feel nothing but sudden loving.

All the world felt the quake, heard the roar,
love was in the air — not only political, but more.
Controversy spread faster than light,
Rome and Egypt — murmuring day and night.

It was love at first sight for Antony,
maybe not so for her —
Still, it bloomed, bloomed ever faster,
strong, beautiful, intelligent, charismatic — both were.

Never easy to divorce Octavian's sister,
to choose an ally, Caesar's once-lover.
Antony risked life and throne,
lived a tiny, but immortal dawn.

Every love has its price to pay,
So, Cleopatra and Antony had theirs that day.
Antony gave himself, for false demise news of her,

the bite of asp took the life of Philopator.

Cleopatra's fury, Antony's guilt,
Cleopatra's retreat, Antony's despair.
Immortal lovers separated by death,
remembered — yet forever united in myth.

THE SOLITUDE OF SORROW

In the happy hours
it was grief accompanied, always.
Now the happy times are over—
Darkness spread near and far.

In these hours of sorrow, the thorn
I wish to feel the happiness all my own.
In a sinking to the depths of ocean,
I will feel the beauty within and lean.

The shooting stars and bright tails
will guide me, to heal me—like pills.
I won't allow anymore, anyone,
to share my happy grief and mourn.

I will fall from a peak unbound
and feel the sky, cloud, and a crash to the ground.
The happy march of my inevitable death
must be felt—none but me on earth.

Never and none should accompany me
when my time of sorrow starts, if I can see.
I won't allow anyone—not even for a moment so brief—
to share my happy moments while I'm in grief.

A MID-SUMMER DAY DREAM

It was just a dream—
Where trees began to scream,
the grasses slithered into snakes,
and bamboos bent into canes.

Leaves turned to alien bugs,
butterflies slipped from my pockets' hugs.
Flowers floated across the lake,
green lights flared from flame and flake.

The plants walked by, shaking hands,
straight lines curled across the lands.
Blooms became dragons in the air,
and hearts broke into iron despair.

A whale morphed into a plane,
mosquitoes marched in a single lane.
Birds turned into drifting kites,
and the sun rose deep in night.

Machines took over all our feelings—
Started sharing love-tale dealings—
whispers spun where silence dwells…
Stories that no one ever tells.

PAIN

Let's have a look
at what we did:
we killed you, my brother,
we killed you, my lover,
I killed them in us.

Let's have a look
at what we are doing,
from the ancient past:
we killed our ancestors,
we killed our nature,
I killed them in us.

I started my own ruin,
I started the game of war,
I killed the happy child,
I killed the unhappy minds,
I bombed Hiroshima,
I buried the rose of my own garden,
I finished Pearl Harbor,
I did it again in Chernobyl,
I ruled over the riots.

How could I do so?
How am I doing so?
Why can't I stop myself?

Because,
I am the gang of I's.

I am you — your friend, and obviously your enemy.

I can fly high,
I can blow fire,
I can catch the sun,
I can make my soul dry,
I am the storage of the "we",
I am the mistake of God,
I am not only a man,
I am men... the hell."

Nothing, Only Pain

No more I can write —
Not a single word, despite
the best of my tries.
Before, it was cries
that shaped themselves into poems so plain;
Now, it's nothing but pain.

No more I can utter.
Back then, it was far better —
Unspoken speeches became poetry,
softly wrapping my wounds and misery.
Now, it's nothing but pain,
no matter how hard I storm my brain.

Stardust Pilgrim

I was traveling over the stardust,
searching for the planet you reside.
I stopped by a supernova at last,
circled by the strongest pull — and abide.

Lost my path in eternity,
reached the planet of tranquility,
Where the pain of losing you was tossed,
no longer haunting me like a ghost.

A place, at last, I have availed —
No emotion, no vow unveiled.
No storm, no breeze,
no shadow, no attachment to freeze.

Among stars that never spoke your name,
I whispered still, and bore the flame.
My voice dissolved in cosmic air,
yet in that silence, I felt you there.

I passed the rings of some planet's might,
and moons that shimmered with silver light.
Each orbit drew me far from grief,
each crater whispered soft relief.

I saw a comet weep and fall,
like memories that once would call.
But in this space, so wide, so bare,
no echo rose — just peace, just air.

I built no temple, drew no line,
no clock to count, no end of time.
Just floating in a velvet sea,
unclaimed, untouched — and finally free.

No map to trace, no need to roam,
I found, at last, a form of home.
Not one of walls or flesh or fire,
but calm beyond all earth's desire.

ALIEN EXPRESSION

No language is rich enough,
no tongue is strong enough,
no lips are capable enough
to express my feelings.
And yet—

I need a new language,
a new alphabet, new pronunciation.
New lips, new tongue—
Far from Earth, born of alien expression.

It must be unique,
like my ache in your absence.
It must be beautiful,
as your eyes are so awfully deep.
It must be unbreakably secure—
no one should decode it.
Let it stay unmorphed, forever.

A Beautiful Moment

Festive voices rose in cheer,
laughter ringing far and near.
A gentle breeze kissed the water's skin
of an ornamental pond, calm within.

Soft shadows danced on quiet streets,
under dim-lit lamps and rhythmic beats.
I took a turn — not meant, but mine —
Toward a path where dark and silence twine.

There you stood, in amber light,
eyes adrift, lost in the night.
Waiting too long for a love delayed,
in that stillness, your sorrow stayed.

I reached for your hand, without a word,
in that hush, no sound was heard.
Pulled you close, just for a while —
A second and a half, a fragile smile.

I remember only that brief embrace,
time stood still in that stolen space.
No words could ever quite express
how much that moment still impresses.

I'll hold it close, never to part —
Forever etched within my heart.

CIGARETTE

When i smoke,
I inhale thou beauty.
At every exhale it increases.
The mist envelope your black hair
with delicate love and care.
The haze, like inescapable web
surrounds your face,
and embellish with elegance.
The radiance of your luminous grace,
is thus irresistible,
I inhale again and again.

Nature as The Messenger

Silent breeze,
originates at the foothill
of beautiful riverbed,
surrounded by not-so-high hills,
covered with green,
touches you,
it travels through the dense,
moves with joy and happiness,
not stopped by the woods,
rather they all, even the animals,
take a sip and smile to see off,
allowing it to flow anywhere and everywhere.

Miles traveled through the windows, highways,
flowers,
no blocked roads, no heartbreak,
nothing could retard her from reaching me.

It comes,
encircles,
envelops,
holds and creates its own path
through my breath.

It settles itself inside
with my every inhale.

Your Happiness is Mine

Somewhere in Dooars, you are,
where air is so fresh,
sun is so scorching.
still, I can feel you happy.
The breeze became my new sense
and Sun became my optical aid.

From afar,
I cherish your jubilant laughter,
nature reminds me —
your happiness is mine.

THE DILEMMA OF DUAL LOVE

Yes
It is true
I am in love with you two..
You both look mesmerizing
and in harmony together.

One of you knew,
but not both of you.
How can I love you together?

Why can't I?
In the world of dilemma
I must be forlorn to secluded hell.

If I could,
I should have broken myself apart into two,
and stayed with both of you.

Now,
I can't afford to lose you either.
In this state of disgrace,
how can I live
or how can I leave
the misery within?

NONE LEFT WITHOUT HOPE

In a deep, lonely forest,
where everything is run by no rule.

Freedom and terror co-exist,
beholding each other.
Trees grow far too rapidly,
and the silence kills broken hearts.
The air stands still,
until the passage is freed
by the fall of a random tree.
No sound of this fall is heard—
no one to hear.
No promises, no one to keep.
No pain, none to suffer.
No fragrance, no one to smell.
At dark, not even animals reside.

Then the phantom whispers
the untold love stories to the river—
the river that flows
through the core of the old forest.

The ancient love between
the roots and the soil,
between the air and the leaves,
between rain and the river,
between the day and the light—
and what not?
Only the dark forest is left alone.

Individual water drops of the stream,
enriched with love and minerals,
clear all the sufferings
of downstream villagers
with hope and health.

You Vanquished Everything of Me

It took thousands of years to weave me.
After that,

I never look back at the beautiful, serene lake,
where the mesmerizing, sacred bloom of lotus floats.

I always overlooked the beauty within,
where bees and breeze fly over an azure basin.

I had sculpted myself thus —
never paid attention to the lovely voices or the music,
never tasted-
the nectar of grapes, old enough to lush.

I forged me to resist myself —
from the captivating earth and all the beauty within.

The ethereal spring was never able to divert me
from my devoir.

Now, it's you —
only you — who vanquished everything,
with a single stroke of brush
on the canvas of my essence.

The past used to fly by so swiftly that now,
I feel suspended in a void of timelessness.

Now,
I can breathe, I can feel, I can see the world anew.
I can live and dream about
every single moment of my voyage.

Perhaps,
it will take an eon
to piece myself back together,
as the person I once used to be.

SEPARATION AND SEPARATION

Shackles binding me alone, longing for nothing.
Separation and separation — increasing day by day.
More and more, distant stars flickering through the
windows.
Deserted for a long period of time, in solitary.

Rain yet to appear, though the envelope of sky is darkest now.
Every bit of work, everything is just procrastinated.
It should have been better, if it was to my heart.
Only stopping by the time was the cure to that longing.

Water bubbles could have showered over me,
With corrosive liquid of tranquility.
That might have healed me — and my soul.
Alas! Walking through the ground, grasses move away.
Over the head, clouds move away.
When I sink my hand in a stream so scenic,
Water's flow turns its direction immediately.

Curse of the universe is thus fatal.
Everything, every rule is overturned — just to punish, not
death.
Only thing sustained is the suffering.
I can't escape these,
Even forgetting the desires I am suffering from.

THE LOST SNOW WHITE

Tiny, Little Girl
I held you tight and firm—
you were dead in my palm,
yet it looked like you had fought
bravely,
longing for life.

Snow-white skin,
beautiful dark eyes…
I can't remember your face precisely,
still, I remember:
your weight,
the clothes you were wrapped in.

I laid you in the graveyard
with bare hands.
I had nothing to do.
I was strong, painless…
Still, no one observed—
not even nature—
the invisible drops of hopelessness
dripping through my eyes,
falling on a beautiful corpse.

Now,
you might be an angel.

Sometimes I mourn
with relentless grief.

Your timeless pose, your silent rest—
they whisper in my memories.
But I never cry.
I know
you fought the toughest battle— life.

Universe

The universe—
perhaps it's more like our brain,
or rather, our heart.
The beautiful stars, at which we gaze,
mesmerized—
perhaps they are scars
on the heart of the universe.

Not at all beautiful,
not at all charming
as they appear to be.
They burn with a million pains,
for zillions of human lifetimes,
before letting go of any one sorrow.

Alas!
Amid the passage of time,
numerous stars of pain are reborn
in the vast alley of dust and emptiness.

The universe within us—
still largely unexplored,
understood by none.

EVERY SHOW MUST GO ON

Days are long and perfect, Lark,
and so are nights—peach-dark.
No calamities are striking long,
day by day, I'm feeling strong.

Soft breeze, soothing sun,
everyone, everywhere, having fun.
Everything feels fit and fine—
Even I appear to shine.

But in this world, so calm and good,
Why am I not in a happy mood?
It's not you who broke me—
Whatever it is, let it be.

Time will pass by overcoming every obstacle.
Nothing can stop the stream of time, no miracles.
If you find me long gone.
Remember- every show must go on.

Love is The Only Reason to Grow

Thus
I became
the bud on a rain tree,
over the naked land of wet leaves,
long fallen on breeze in a spring evening.

Cherished by the soft sun,
loved by the air and water,
now I am green.

Soon I will become the pink —
happy to dream that
in coming week
I might fill your heart
with marvelous joy and happiness.

I am trying to embrace myself
for your eyes only.
I will swing in the latent air
for your attention only.

One day, I will pluck myself and fall
in the hidden desire of ethereal incidents.
That incident might allow me to fall on you.
Will you pick and keep?

Love With a Fall

Without deciduous trees,
a season is not a spring.

Without failing to achieve your desire,
a desire is not a desire.

Without the chance of defeat,
no battle is worth the triumph.

Without tremendous sufferings,
no achievement is etched as great.

Often, the worst sufferers of time
are engraved in its cycle—
with memories that sparkle.

Love, without a fall,
is not love at all.

"Why do we die? To make life precious…"-somewhere in the vacuum"

You are so beautiful. You may be ugly either. You are the richest person on earth or the poorest one. You may be the happiest person on earth or the Saddest of the universe. Whoever you may be or whatever your race is, you are going to die. Yes, you are going to die, even if you are not a human the story is the same. It may come today or tomorrow or the long after, but you can't escape from it. You were been issued with a death certificate, which is to be dated. This is just not a truth, it is also the mystery that we are living for the time being. We come, we play a role and pass by. It hurts, but can't be avoided. Whoever we may be, we can't skip the pain of death. Who is going to get hurt when your life is going to be unearthed? Maybe a lot of people, who love you, who live you, who circles you. But the real question is who is the worst sufferer? Believe it or not, it may be pathetic to lose the nearest ones. But losing self is the hardest one and the emptiness of self-extinction remains forever and after. You die, your dreams die, those dreams no one ever listened to, your senses die, which no one could sense ever. Your feeling dies. Which no one could feel either. Most importantly your curiosity to know the unknown dies before you acquire the knowledge. The dead one can never live in the future. They don't know whatever is going on here on this planet or those supernovae. Life has an end but death doesn't. And saddest part remains with the question: Why did I come to life?